Unlock the Power of Fiction Writing with AI: A Comprehensive Guide to Crafting Compelling Stories
By Justin Hoke

This book is dedicated to Richard Hoke, My Grandpa. He inspired me to strive to be my best self, to go after my dreams, and never give up. It was his collection of fiction novels by the likes of Donald Clayton Porter, Louis L'Amour, and Zane Grey that first got me interested in the world of fiction writing.

Contents:

Introduction:

Welcome to "The Art of Prompt Engineering: A Guide to Crafting Compelling Fiction Stories". If you're passionate about writing and eager to learn the techniques that can take your writing to the next level, you've come to the right place. Whether you're a seasoned writer or just starting out, this guide will provide you with the tools and insights you need to craft stories that captivate your readers and leave a lasting impression.

Prompt engineering is a term that refers to the process of using prompts or story starters to generate ideas and help you get started with your writing. The goal of this guide is to show you how to take these prompts and turn them into full-fledged fiction stories that are both compelling and memorable.

We'll begin by exploring the building blocks of storytelling, from creating unique concepts and memorable characters to establishing conflict and tension. You'll learn how to use setting to enhance your story, incorporate dialogue and interior monologue, and build suspense to heighten emotional impact. We'll delve into the art of plotting your story arc and developing a strong narrative voice, and you'll learn how to balance show and tell in your writing to keep your readers engaged.

Along the way, you'll also pick up tips and techniques for crafting compelling dialogue, enhancing your writing through symbolism and subtext, revising and polishing your work, and preparing your work for publication. Whatever your starting point, this guide will provide you with the guidance and inspiration you need to bring your writing to life.

So let's get started!

Chapter 1: Introduction to Prompt Engineering

Have you ever found yourself staring at a blank screen, struggling to come up with a story idea? Or maybe you have a great idea, but you're not quite sure how to turn it into a full-fledged fiction story? If so, you're not alone. Many writers experience these challenges, but the good news is that there's a solution: prompt engineering.

Prompt engineering is a technique that leverages the power of AI to help writers generate story ideas and overcome writer's block. It involves using prompts or story starters as a starting point, then building on those prompts to create full-fledged fiction stories.

Whether you're a seasoned writer or just starting out, prompt engineering can help you take your writing to the next level.

But what exactly is a prompt, and how does it work? Simply put, a prompt is a prompt or question that is designed to inspire creative thinking and generate story ideas. These prompts can take many forms, from a simple word or phrase to a complex scenario. The idea is to use the prompt as a starting point and let your imagination run wild.

So, how does AI fit into the equation? AI algorithms can analyze large volumes of text to determine patterns and correlations that are not immediately apparent to the human eye. This allows AI to generate new story ideas and prompts that are both relevant and unique.

For example, you might start with a prompt such as "A detective who can see into the future." From there, you can build a story around this character, exploring their unique abilities and the challenges they face as they use their powers to solve crimes. The possibilities are endless, and the best part is that you don't have to do it all on your own. AI algorithms can help you generate new ideas and keep your creative juices flowing.

But that's not all. AI can also help you with other aspects of your writing, such as character development, plot structure, and dialogue. By using AI to analyze your writing and identify areas for improvement, you can take your writing to the next level and create stories that captivate your readers.

So, why not give prompt engineering a try? Whether you're an aspiring writer or a seasoned pro, this technique can help you unleash your imagination and bring your stories to life. So what are you waiting for? Start experimenting with prompts today and see where your imagination takes you!

Chapter 2: Understanding the Building Blocks of Storytelling

To become a successful fiction writer, it's important to understand the building blocks of storytelling. These building blocks are the elements that make up a story, including characters, plot, setting, theme, and more. By understanding these elements and how they work together, you can create stories that are both engaging and impactful.

So, what are the building blocks of storytelling? Let's take a closer look at each one.

Characters: Characters are the people or creatures that populate your story. They are the ones who drive the action and experience the events of the story. To create compelling characters, it's important to think about who they are, what they want, and what they're willing to do to get it.

Plot: Plot is the sequence of events that make up your story. It's the foundation upon which your characters and setting are built. A good plot is one that is both engaging and believable, and it should keep your reader hooked from beginning to end.

Setting: Setting is the environment in which your story takes place. It can be a real place, like New York City, or it can be a fictional world, like Middle Earth. The setting provides the backdrop for your story and can help to establish mood and atmosphere.

Theme: Theme is the underlying message or idea that runs throughout your story. It's what your story is ultimately about, and it's what gives it meaning. To create stories with impact, it's important to think about what you want to say and how you want to say it.

These are just a few of the building blocks of storytelling. By understanding these elements and how they work together, you can create stories that are both engaging and impactful. But how do you put these building blocks together to create a story? That's where AI comes in.

AI algorithms can analyze large volumes of text to determine the most effective combinations of building blocks. This allows AI to generate new and innovative story ideas that are based on proven formulas and structures. Whether you're looking to create a classic hero's journey or a contemporary romance, AI can help you find the right building blocks to make your story a success.

So, now that you have a basic understanding of the building blocks of storytelling, why not give AI a try? With its ability to generate new and innovative story ideas, AI can help you take your writing to the next level and create stories that will captivate your readers. So what are you waiting for? Start experimenting

with AI today and see where
your imagination takes you!

Chapter 3: Developing Unique Story Concepts

Once you understand the building blocks of storytelling, it's time to start thinking about your own story concepts. But where do you begin? How do you come up with ideas that are unique and engaging? That's where AI can help.

With its ability to analyze large volumes of text and data, AI can generate new and innovative story concepts based on proven formulas and structures. It can help you find unique combinations of characters, settings, and themes that will make your story stand out.

But AI is just a tool, and it's up to you to use it in the most effective way possible. Here are a few tips to help you get started:

Know your audience: Before you start generating ideas, it's important to know who you're writing for. Who is your target audience, and what do they want to read about? Understanding your audience will help you generate ideas that are relevant and appealing to them.

Think outside the box: While AI can generate new and innovative ideas, it's up to you to think outside the box and put your own spin on them. Ask yourself, "What if?" and "What would happen if?" These questions can help you take your ideas in new and unexpected directions.

Don't be afraid to experiment: Experimentation is key to developing unique story concepts. Don't be afraid to try new things and push the boundaries of what's possible. You never know what you might come up with!

By following these tips and using AI to generate new and innovative ideas, you can develop unique and engaging story concepts that will capture your reader's attention and keep them hooked from beginning to end. So why not give it a try? The possibilities are endless!

Chapter 4: Creating Compelling Characters

Characters are the heart and soul of your story. They drive the action, evoke emotions, and bring your story to life. That's why it's so important to create characters that are both compelling and relatable. And that's where AI can help.

With its ability to analyze large volumes of text and data, AI can generate character profiles and suggest unique traits, motivations, and backgrounds that will make your characters stand out. It can also help you develop characters that are consistent and believable, so your readers will feel invested in their journeys.

But creating compelling characters is more than just filling in a list of traits. Here are a few tips to help you get started:

Know your characters: Before you start writing, take the time to get to know your characters. What motivates them? What are their fears and desires? What makes them unique? Understanding your characters will help you bring them to life on the page.

Show, don't tell: Instead of telling your readers what your characters are like, show them through their actions and dialogue. This will help you build empathy and connection with your readers.

Give your characters flaws: No one is perfect, and neither should your characters. Give them flaws and weaknesses that make them human and relatable. Your readers will appreciate the authenticity.

Make them active: Your characters should be driving the action, not just reacting to it. Give them goals and obstacles that they need to overcome. This will keep your story moving and make your characters more dynamic.

Let them evolve: Characters should change and grow over the course of your story. This will keep your readers engaged and invested in their journeys.

By using AI to generate character profiles and following these tips, you can create characters that are both compelling and relatable. And that's what will keep your readers turning the pages, eager to find out what happens next. So why not give it a try? Your characters are waiting to be brought to life!

Chapter 5: Establishing Conflict and Tension

Conflict and tension are the driving forces behind a good story. They keep your readers engaged, on the edge of their seats, and wondering what will happen next. But how do you create conflict and tension in your story? And how can AI help?

Conflict can come in many forms, from internal struggles to external battles. It can be between characters, or between a character and society, or even between a character and their own fears and desires. Conflict is what keeps your story interesting and drives your characters forward.

Tension, on the other hand, is the feeling of unease or uncertainty that comes from the conflict. It's what keeps your readers engaged and invested in your story. The higher the tension, the more your readers will want to know what happens next.

Here are a few tips to help you create conflict and tension in your story:

Start with the problem: Every good story starts with a problem that your characters need to solve. This problem should be the source of your conflict and tension.

Raise the stakes: The more important the problem, the higher the stakes, and the more tension there will be. So make sure your characters have a lot to lose if they don't solve the problem.

Create obstacles: Your characters shouldn't be able to solve the problem easily. They need obstacles that make it difficult, and that's what creates tension.

Build momentum: Tension builds as your characters get closer to solving the problem. So make sure to increase the tension throughout your story.

Make it personal: Conflict and tension are more interesting when they are personal and directly affect your characters. So make sure your characters have a personal stake in solving the problem.

AI can help you create conflict and tension in your story by analyzing large volumes of text and data. It can suggest unique obstacles, raise the stakes, and help you build momentum. And by using AI, you can create conflict and tension that is both surprising and engaging, so your readers will be on the edge of their seats from start to finish.

But remember, conflict and tension are just two pieces of the puzzle. They are important, but they are not enough to make a good story. You also need a compelling plot, well-developed characters, and a clear narrative structure. So while AI can help you create conflict and tension, don't forget to focus on the other elements of your story as well.

With a strong focus on conflict and tension, your story will be more engaging, more interesting, and more likely to keep your readers coming back for more. So why not give it a try? Your readers are waiting!

Chapter 6: Using Setting to Enhance Your Story

The setting of your story can be just as important as the characters and events that take place within it. A well-crafted setting can provide a backdrop that both informs and enriches your story, giving it a sense of place and a deeper meaning. Whether you're writing about a futuristic world or a small town in the Midwest, the setting of your story can have a profound impact on the way your readers experience it.

One of the most effective ways to use AI in your writing is to create detailed and compelling settings. You can use AI tools to generate descriptions of landscapes, cities, and buildings, giving you a rich and immersive world to work with. Additionally, AI can help you create maps and diagrams of your world, allowing you to visualize your setting and develop a deeper understanding of it.

To use setting effectively in your story, it's important to keep a few key concepts in mind. First, think about the mood and atmosphere you want to create. A dark, brooding cityscape will have a very different feel than a bright and bustling beach town. Second, consider the characters who inhabit your setting and how they interact with it. A character who is struggling to survive in a harsh and unforgiving world will have a very different relationship to their environment than one who is living in a lush and thriving city.

Another important aspect of setting is pacing. Just as the events in your story can create tension and suspense, the settings you choose can play a crucial role in how quickly your story moves along. If you're writing a fast-paced action story, for example, you might choose a city that is always in motion, with characters racing from one location to the next. On the other hand, if you're writing a slow-burning mystery, you might choose a small town with winding streets and hidden alleys, where secrets are lurking around every corner.

Finally, don't be afraid to use your setting to reflect the themes and messages of your story. For example, a polluted city might be a metaphor for a corrupted society, while a lush, natural landscape might symbolize the hope and renewal that is possible in the world.

In short, setting is an incredibly powerful tool in fiction writing. By using AI to help you create vivid and detailed settings, you can bring your stories to life in new and exciting ways. Whether you're exploring a futuristic cityscape or a small town in the countryside, your readers will be drawn into your world and captivated by the stories you tell.

Chapter 7: Incorporating Dialogue and Interior Monologue

Incorporating dialogue and interior monologue into a story is crucial in creating depth, revealing character, and building tension. It's a vital tool in fiction writing that helps bring a story to life.

In fiction writing, dialogue refers to the conversation between characters in a story. The words spoken by characters can provide insight into their personality, motives, and conflicts. It can also be used to convey information, establish relationships between characters, and move the plot forward.

Interior monologue refers to the thoughts and feelings of a character that are revealed to the reader. It provides a deeper understanding of a character's inner world and allows the reader to experience their thoughts, emotions, and motivations.

To use dialogue and interior monologue effectively, it's crucial to remember that both should serve the story. The words spoken and thoughts revealed should reveal character, advance the plot, and create tension.

The use of dialogue and interior monologue should be balanced with other elements of a story, such as description and action. Too much dialogue or interior monologue can make a story feel flat, while too little can leave characters feeling one-dimensional.

When it comes to writing dialogue, it's important to remember that characters should sound different from each other. Their speech patterns, dialects, and vocal tones should be unique to them and help reveal their personality.

Interior monologue, on the other hand, should be written in a way that allows the reader to experience the character's thoughts and emotions. It should be written in the character's voice and reflect their unique perspective.

Incorporating dialogue and interior monologue is a

challenge, but with practice and attention to detail, it can be mastered. And with the help of AI, writers can now use prompts and suggestions to help them create dynamic and engaging conversations and inner thoughts for their characters.

The goal of this chapter is to give you the tools you need to effectively use dialogue and interior monologue in your writing. With a little practice, you'll be able to create dynamic and compelling stories that will keep your readers engaged and invested.

Chapter 8: Building Suspense and Heightening Emotional Impact

As writers, our ultimate goal is to engage and captivate our readers, and one way to do that is by building suspense and heightening emotional impact in our stories. Suspense and emotion are powerful tools in a writer's toolkit, and when used effectively, can greatly enhance the overall reading experience for the reader.

One way to build suspense is through the use of foreshadowing. Foreshadowing is a literary device that gives the reader hints or clues about events that are yet to happen in the story. This not only creates anticipation and excitement, but it also helps the reader to make connections and understand the story on a deeper level.

Another way to build suspense is through the use of tension. Tension is created when the reader is aware of an impending danger or conflict, and they are unsure of how the protagonist will handle it. The tension in a story can be heightened by using elements such as pacing, point of view, and description.

Emotional impact, on the other hand, is achieved through the creation of empathy between the reader and the characters. The reader needs to care about what is happening to the characters in the story in order for them to be emotionally invested. To create this empathy, writers often use character development, internal conflict, and relationships.

Using AI to help with the building of suspense and heightening of emotional impact is not limited to simply suggesting plot twists and turns. AI can also be used to analyze and provide feedback on the pacing, tone, and overall emotional impact of a story. For example, if a story lacks tension, AI could suggest increasing the pace or adjusting the point of view to create a more intense experience for the reader.

In conclusion, suspense and emotional impact are important elements in fiction writing, and AI can be a valuable tool for writers looking to enhance these aspects of their stories. By using

AI to analyze pacing, tone, and character development, writers can create stories that are not only exciting and engaging, but also emotionally resonant with their readers.

Chapter 9: Plotting Your Story Arc

As you dive deeper into the world of fiction writing, it becomes increasingly clear that every great story has a well-constructed arc. It's the backbone of your story, the path that takes your reader on a journey from beginning to end. Without a solid arc, your story may feel aimless and unfulfilling to your reader.

So what exactly is a story arc? Simply put, it's the structure that guides the development of your plot and characters. The traditional story arc includes five key elements: setup, rising action, climax, falling action, and resolution.

The setup is where you introduce your characters, world, and premise. This stage is crucial as it sets the stage for the rest of your story.

The rising action is where the story really starts to take shape. Conflicts arise, challenges are faced, and your characters are tested. It's the part of the story that keeps the reader turning the pages, as the stakes continue to rise and the tension builds.

The climax is the turning point, where everything comes to a head. The fate of your characters, and often the world they inhabit, will be determined at this point.

The falling action is where the aftermath of the climax is explored and the consequences of the characters' actions are revealed.

Finally, the resolution brings the story to a close, tying up loose ends and offering closure to the reader.

Creating a story arc is one of the most challenging and rewarding aspects of writing fiction. With the help of AI, you can explore different story arcs and plot structures, testing different scenarios and getting a fresh perspective on your work. Whether you're a seasoned writer or just starting out, incorporating AI into your writing process can help you take your storytelling to the next level.

One of the greatest benefits of AI in this context is that it allows you to see your story from different angles, helping you identify patterns, themes, and areas for improvement. With its advanced algorithms and language models, AI can help you craft a more sophisticated and impactful story arc.

As you develop your own unique story arc, remember that there are no hard and fast rules. Every great story is different, and what works for one writer may not work for another. The important thing is to be open to new possibilities and embrace the power of AI to help you unleash your full creative potential. With a solid story arc and a willingness to experiment, you can write a story that will captivate and inspire your readers.

Chapter 10: Developing a Strong Narrative Voice

As you delve deeper into your fiction writing journey, it's important to cultivate a strong and unique narrative voice. Your narrative voice is the distinct style and tone you use to tell your story, and it's what sets your writing apart from the countless other voices in the crowded world of literature.

But what exactly is a narrative voice, and how can you develop one that's both powerful and original? In this chapter, we'll explore the various elements that make up a narrative voice and offer tips for refining your own.

First, it's important to understand that your narrative voice is more than just the words you choose to write. It's the sum of all the choices you make as a writer, from your sentence structure and pacing to your character development and dialogue. Essentially, your narrative voice is the lens through which your reader experiences your story.

So how do you create a strong and distinctive narrative voice? The key is to embrace your unique perspective and experiences, and let them inform your writing. Think about the books, movies, and TV shows that you love, and try to identify what makes their voices so compelling. Then, experiment with incorporating some of those elements into your own writing.

For example, maybe you're drawn to writing that's heavy on sensory detail and imagery. In that case, you might try incorporating more vivid descriptions of your setting and characters into your own writing. Or perhaps you're drawn to a more reserved, introspective style. In that case, you might experiment with writing in first-person and incorporating more interior monologue into your storytelling.

Another important aspect of narrative voice is tone. Tone refers to the overall mood or feeling of your writing, and it can be influenced by a variety of factors, including your characters, setting, and plot. To develop a strong and consistent tone, it's important to be intentional about the emotions you want to evoke in your readers. Think about what you want them to feel as they read your story, and work to infuse that feeling into every aspect of your writing, from your dialogue to your descriptions.

Finally, it's important to remember that developing a strong narrative voice takes time and practice. Don't be discouraged if you don't feel like you've found your voice right away. Keep writing and experimenting, and eventually, you'll find the voice that feels most natural and authentic to you.

Now, let's take a look at how you can use AI to help you refine and strengthen your narrative voice. One of the biggest benefits of using AI for fiction writing is that it can help you generate new ideas and perspectives that you may not have considered on your own. For example, you can use AI-powered writing prompts to help you experiment with different styles and tones, or use AI-powered character generators to help you create more complex and dynamic characters.

Additionally, AI can help you identify patterns and themes in your writing that you may not have been aware of. For example, you can use AI-powered text analysis tools to analyze your writing and identify your most common narrative devices, or use AI-powered sentiment analysis tools to determine the overall tone of your writing.

By leveraging the power of AI, you can not only develop a more refined and compelling narrative voice, but also gain a deeper understanding of your own writing style and tendencies. So whether you're a seasoned author or just starting out on your fiction writing journey, AI can be a valuable tool for helping you achieve your goals and bring your stories to life.

Chapter 11: Balancing Show and Tell in Your Writing

As a fiction writer, it is important to strike a balance between showing and telling in your writing. Showing refers to the use of descriptive language and actions to let the reader experience the story, while telling refers to the use of direct explanations and narrations.

Too much telling can make your writing feel flat and dull, while too much showing can slow down the pace of your story and bog down the reader with excessive detail. Striking a balance between the two is crucial to create an engaging, relatable, and impactful story.

One effective way to balance show and tell is to use a combination of sensory language and dialogue to bring your characters and setting to life. For example, instead of simply telling the reader that a character is sad, you can show their sadness through their body language, tone of voice, or thoughts.

Interior monologue can also be used to balance show and tell in your writing. By allowing the reader to get inside the head of your characters, you can provide a deeper understanding of their emotions, motivations, and inner thoughts. This technique can help you show the reader what your characters are feeling, rather than simply telling them.

It's also important to keep in mind the pace of your story when balancing show and tell. In fast-paced action scenes, it's best to keep the descriptions short and to the point, while in slower, more introspective scenes, you can afford to be more descriptive.

As you work on balancing show and tell in your writing, it can be helpful to get feedback from beta readers or to have your work critiqued by other writers. They can provide valuable insights into whether you are striking the right balance and where you can improve.

Finally, remember that balancing show and tell is a process and will likely change as your writing evolves. With practice and experience, you'll find your own unique style that works best for you and your writing goals.

By keeping the importance of balancing show and tell in mind, and by using a combination of sensory language, dialogue, interior monologue, and pacing, you can create a story that is both engaging and impactful. And with the help of AI, you can further enhance your writing by using its advanced analysis capabilities to identify areas where you can improve your show and tell balance. Whether you're a seasoned writer or just starting out, incorporating AI into your writing process can help take your storytelling to the next level.

Chapter 12: Crafting Compelling Dialogue

Dialogue is a vital component of storytelling that adds depth and dimension to your characters and contributes to the overall flow of your story. It can also serve as a powerful tool for building suspense, heightening emotional impact, and advancing the plot. In this chapter, we'll explore the elements of great dialogue and how you can use AI to help you craft compelling conversations that will engage and captivate your readers.

First and foremost, great dialogue should sound natural and authentic. People don't talk in perfectly formed sentences or with complete thoughts; they use colloquialisms, filler words, and nonverbal cues to communicate. To achieve a realistic and believable quality to your dialogue, it's important to pay attention to the way people actually speak and incorporate those nuances into your writing.

One way to do this is by using AI to analyze real-world dialogue. By feeding AI large amounts of transcribed conversations, it can learn to recognize the patterns and rhythms of natural speech and use that information to generate believable dialogue for your characters.

Another important aspect of great dialogue is its ability to reveal character. Characters should have their own unique vocal patterns, mannerisms, and speech patterns that reveal their personalities, motivations, and inner conflicts. By using AI to analyze your characters' dialogue, you can identify patterns and tendencies in the way they speak and use those insights to further develop their personalities and make your dialogue more dynamic and engaging.

Additionally, great dialogue should also be tense and dynamic. It should reveal new information, advance the plot, and create conflict and tension between characters. By using AI to analyze the dialogue in your story, you can identify areas where you can increase tension and conflict and make your dialogue more engaging and captivating.

One way to do this is by using AI to identify and highlight opportunities for subtext. Subtext refers to the underlying meaning or emotion behind what a character is saying. By using AI to analyze your characters' dialogue, you can identify when a character's words don't match their tone or body language, which can reveal deeper conflicts or tensions that can be explored in your writing.

Finally, great dialogue should be concise and to the point. Long-winded or repetitive dialogue can slow down the pace of your story and distract from the plot. By using AI to analyze the length and structure of your dialogue, you can identify areas where you can tighten and streamline your writing to make it more effective and engaging.

In conclusion, crafting compelling dialogue is an essential part of storytelling that can add depth and dimension to your characters, build suspense and tension, and advance the plot. By using AI to analyze and generate dialogue, you can ensure that your conversations sound natural and authentic, reveal character, and are concise and dynamic. With these tools, you'll be well on your way to crafting captivating stories that will keep your readers hooked from beginning to end.

Chapter 13: Enhancing Your Writing Through Symbolism and Subtext

Symbolism and subtext are powerful tools for writers, allowing them to add depth and meaning to their stories. These elements are especially useful for writers looking to create a sense of mystery, suspense, or emotional impact. By using symbols and subtext, writers can convey complex ideas and emotions without explicitly stating them.

Symbolism is the use of objects, images, or actions that represent something beyond their literal meaning. For example, a snake could symbolize danger or temptation, while a white dove might symbolize peace or hope.

By incorporating symbols into your writing, you can convey a deeper meaning to your readers and create a more immersive experience.

Subtext, on the other hand, refers to the underlying meaning or messages in a story that are not explicitly stated. This can be achieved through dialogue, inner thoughts, and actions of the characters. For example, if two characters are talking about the weather, the subtext could be their hidden feelings or motivations. By including subtext in your writing, you can add depth to your characters and build suspense by leaving things unsaid.

When using symbolism and subtext, it is important to be

subtle and not overuse these elements. Overloading your story with symbols and subtext can make it confusing for your readers and detract from the overall experience. Instead, choose symbols and subtext that are relevant to your story and use them sparingly and effectively.

AI can be a valuable tool in helping writers develop and incorporate symbols and subtext into their writing. With the ability to analyze large amounts of data and identify patterns, AI can help writers identify the best symbols and subtext to use in their stories. Additionally, AI can provide suggestions on how to incorporate these elements into their writing in a way that is both effective and subtle.

For example, if a writer is creating a story about a character who is struggling with addiction, they might use the symbol of a snake to represent the dangerous and alluring nature of the addiction. The subtext could be the character's internal struggle as they try to overcome their addiction. With the help of AI, the writer can analyze different symbols and subtext to determine which ones are the most effective in conveying the intended message.

In conclusion, incorporating symbolism and subtext into your writing can greatly enhance the depth and meaning of your story. These elements allow writers to convey complex ideas and emotions in a subtle and effective way. By utilizing AI, writers can identify the most effective symbols and subtext to incorporate into their stories and create a more immersive and impactful reading experience for their readers.

Chapter 14: Revising and Polishing Your Work

Writing is a process and even the best authors have to revise and edit their work multiple times before it is ready for publication. As you write, you'll become more aware of what works and what doesn't work in your story, and your writing will improve as a result. And while the idea of revising and editing can be daunting, it can also be incredibly rewarding. With the right tools and approach, you can take your writing to the next level, making it both more polished and more powerful.

One of the most important aspects of revising and polishing your work is being able to take a step back from your writing and look at it objectively. This can be difficult, as you've likely become very attached to your work, but it is essential if you want to make your writing the best it can be. To do this, try reading your work out loud, or if possible, have someone else read it to you. This can help you identify areas that need improvement, and you can make the necessary changes.

Another important aspect of revising and polishing your work is to focus on character development. Make sure that each character has a distinct voice and personality, and that their motivations and actions are clear. If a character's motivations and actions are unclear, it can make the story confusing for the reader, and detract from the overall experience. Take the time to really think about your characters and how they would react in different situations.

In addition to character development, pay close attention to the pacing of your story. Make sure that it flows well and that there are no abrupt jumps or slowdowns in the action. A well-paced story will keep the reader engaged, and prevent boredom or frustration. You can also consider adding in plot twists, cliffhangers, or other dramatic events to keep the reader engaged and on the edge of their seat.

When it comes to dialogue, it's important to make sure that it sounds natural and authentic. Avoid using language or expressions that feel forced or artificial, and instead, aim for dialogue that feels like a conversation that could actually take place. It's also important to be mindful of the tone of the dialogue, and to make sure that it fits the tone of the scene. For example, if a character is feeling sad or upset, their dialogue should reflect that emotion.

Finally, consider using AI tools to help you revise and polish your work. These tools can provide you with feedback on areas such as grammar, spelling, and punctuation, and can help you identify areas where you can improve your writing. They can also provide you with suggestions on how to rephrase sentences or paragraphs to make your writing more powerful and effective.

In conclusion, revising and polishing your work is an important step in the writing process, and can help you take your writing to the next level. By taking a step back, focusing on character development and pacing, making sure your dialogue sounds natural, and using AI tools, you can create a story that is both polished and powerful.

Chapter 15: Preparing Your Work for Publication

As a fiction writer, the ultimate goal is to share your work with the world. But before you do that, it's important to ensure that your story is the best it can be. Preparation is key when it comes to publishing your work, and with the help of AI, you can take your writing to the next level.

The first step in preparing your work for publication is to revise and edit your writing. This process can be time-consuming, but it's essential to ensure that your story is polished and ready for readers. AI tools like grammar and spell checkers can help you catch any typos or errors in your writing. However, it's still important to read your work carefully and make revisions by hand.

Once your writing is polished, you need to think about formatting. Proper formatting is important to ensure that your work is easy to read and looks professional. AI tools can help you format your work, but it's important to make sure that the formatting is consistent and that your work meets industry standards.

Next, consider how you want to share your work with the world. There are several options for publishing your work, including traditional publishers, self-publishing, or e-book publishing. Each of these options has its own advantages and disadvantages, and it's important to choose the one that's right for you and your work.

Traditional publishing involves submitting your work to a publisher for consideration. If the publisher is interested in your work, they will offer you a contract and take care of the publishing process for you. This option is often the best choice for new writers, as publishers can provide you with exposure and marketing resources. However, the downside of traditional publishing is that it can be difficult to get your work accepted and the process can be slow.

Self-publishing involves taking care of the publishing process yourself. This option gives you more control over the final product and allows you to publish your work quickly. However, it also requires more work on your part and you'll have to take care of marketing and distribution on your own.

E-book publishing involves publishing your work as an e-book, which can be sold through online retailers like Amazon. This option is a good choice if you want to reach a wide audience quickly, as e-books can be easily downloaded and read on a variety of devices. However, it's important to make sure that your e-book is formatted correctly and that it meets industry standards.

Finally, it's important to consider copyright protection. Copyright laws protect your work from being copied or used without your permission. You can register your work with the Copyright Office to ensure that your rights are protected.

In conclusion, preparing your work for publication is an important step in the writing process. With the help of AI, you can ensure that your work is polished and ready for readers. Consider your options for publishing, format your work correctly, and take steps to protect your rights. By doing so, you'll be well on your way to sharing your work with the world and becoming a successful fiction writer.

Chapter 16: Helping Others through Sharing

Congratulations, you have made it to the end of our journey through the world of fiction writing and AI. I hope that you have found the information and guidance provided in these pages to be valuable and helpful. But our work doesn't stop here!

I want to encourage you to share this book with others who may also benefit from its wisdom. Perhaps you know someone who is struggling with writing fiction, or maybe you simply have a friend who is passionate about storytelling. In either case, this book can be a game-changer for them.

By sharing this book with others, you are not only helping your friends, but also yourself. You are part of a community of writers and storytellers who are always looking to improve their skills and reach new heights. When you share this book, you are sharing a piece of that community and helping others to join you on your journey.

Of course, sharing this book is also a great way to support the author and publishers who have put so much time and effort into creating this valuable resource. By giving this book as a gift, you are making a tangible contribution to the world of fiction writing and helping to ensure that the author and publishers can continue to

create works that will inspire
and inform future generations.

So what are you waiting for?
Spread the word about this book
to everyone you know. Leave a
review on Amazon, Goodreads,
or any other platform that you
use. And if you really believe in
the message of this book,
consider buying a few extra
copies to give away as gifts to
friends, family, and fellow
writers.

Together, we can make a real
difference in the world of fiction
writing. Let's get started!

Appendix: Example Prompts to Help You Communicate Better with AI

Here are some examples of fiction writing prompts with the right amount of information to write fiction according to the important principles discussed in this book:

"Write a short story about a character who is trying to escape from a dangerous situation in a dark and creepy forest. Use setting to enhance the emotional impact and suspense of the story."

"Write a story about a character who is torn between their loyalty to their family and their love for someone else. Use dialogue and interior monologue to show the character's inner conflicts and emotional journey."

"Write a story about a character who is struggling to come to terms with a tragedy that has impacted their life. Use symbolism and subtext to show the character's emotions and journey towards healing."

"Write a story about a detective who is trying to solve a mystery. Use plot twists and foreshadowing to build suspense and keep the reader engaged."

"Write a story about a character who is on a journey of self-discovery. Use a strong narrative voice to show the character's perspective and emotional journey."

"Write a story about two characters who have opposing beliefs but find common ground through a shared experience. Use a balanced approach of show and tell to bring the story to life."

"Write a story about a character who is trying to find their place in the world. Use vivid descriptions and sensory details to help the reader connect with the character's experiences."

"Write a story about a character who is faced with a difficult decision. Use a well-crafted plot to show the character's journey towards making the right choice."

"Write a story about a character who overcomes an obstacle. Use vivid dialogue to help the reader connect with the character's emotions and experiences."

These prompts provide the AI with enough information to write fiction that incorporates the key principles discussed in the book, such as setting, dialogue, narrative voice, plot, suspense, and character development.

Finally, there is no magic prompt that will cause AI to write amazing fiction in the style of some of the world's best fiction writers. AI writing is limited by the data it was trained on and the algorithms used to generate the text. It is important to provide a clear prompt with specific information and guidelines to guide the AI, but ultimately the final result will depend on the quality and diversity of the training data, the complexity of the algorithms, and the skill of the person using it. To create compelling fiction, it's important to have a deep understanding of the elements of storytelling, such as plot, character, setting, dialogue, voice, and style, and to continually revise and polish your work.